# OLD-TIME CIRCUS CUTS

## A PICTORIAL ARCHIVE OF 202 ILLUSTRATIONS

Edited by

## CHARLES PHILIP FOX

Dover Publications, Inc.
New York

# ACKNOWLEDGEMENTS

The publisher and editor wish to thank the Circus World Museum, Baraboo, Wisconsin 53913, and its Chief Librarian and Historian, Robert L. Parkinson, for the use of 76 engravings from their files among the 202 presented in this collection.

Published in Canada by General Publishing Company, Ltd., 30 Lesmill Road, Don Mills, Toronto, Ontario.
Published in the United Kingdom by Constable and Company, Ltd., 10 Orange Street, London WC2H 7EG.

*Old-Time Circus Cuts: A Pictorial Archive of 202 Illustrations*, is a new work, first published by Dover Publications, Inc., in 1979.

DOVER *Pictorial Archive* SERIES

*Old-Time Circus Cuts: A Pictorial Archive of 202 Illustrations* belongs to the Dover Pictorial Archive Series. Up to ten illustrations may be used on any one project or in any single publication, free and without special permission. Wherever possible, include a credit line indicating the title of this book, author and publisher. Please address the publisher for permission to make more extensive use of illustrations in this book than that authorized above.
The reproduction of this book in whole is prohibited.

*International Standard Book Number: 0-486-23653-6*
*Library of Congress Catalog Card Number: 79-50262*

Manufactured in the United States of America
Dover Publications, Inc.
180 Varick Street
New York, N.Y. 10014

# INTRODUCTION

Circus advertising has always been in a class all its own. The very word "circus" conjures up in everyone's imagination an entire series of happenings, some of which are thrilling, others graceful, comic, beautiful, breathtaking, elegant, ponderous and even wondrous. It was the job of commercial artists working on circus accounts to portray all these facets. Their drawings filled the pages of tens of thousands of printed heralds, couriers, programs, hangers, snipes and dodgers, building excitement from the first announcement of the coming of the circus to circus day itself. This book reproduces outstanding examples of their work. The earliest cuts date from around 1880, when there were about 35 circuses traveling the country; many more date from the grand era circa 1900, when there were about 75 traveling circuses; and a few date from as recent as 1950, when slightly more than 40 circuses were in operation.

To supply the advertising art for these circuses, the great lithographing establishments maintained retinues of artists, most of whom had special skills. Some were superb at drawing wild animals, some had talent for drawing horses, others were experts at drawing people, and so forth. There were also artists who specialized entirely in lettering. (In addition to black-and-white work, the lithography studios produced posters for the circuses. Some of the finest examples are presented in *American Circus Posters in Full Color*, Dover 23693-5.)

Because of the similarity of types of circus acts, the printers standardized their artwork. It was only the huge, wealthy railroad circuses that could afford art specifically commissioned for their featured acts. The many smaller shows were very pleased with the availability of stock or standard engravings, which reduced the cost of their printed matter.

Printers ran proofs of the myriad engravings in their stock, and sent the sheets to the press agents of the various circuses. The agents cut out the engravings they wanted and pasted them up into a dummy which they returned, along with the written copy to be set in type and printed. The printer was thus able to give the press agent or circus owner exactly what he wanted.

This procedure meant that many shows might be using the same engravings in their advertising. In any given year, however, these circuses were fanned out across the country and, because their routes usually did not conflict, there was no harm done if a number of shows used the same artwork. After all, the engravings were merely meant to indicate the types of acts a show had. The dog-and-pony shows would not be likely to use engravings of aerial acts. If two or three shows each had a rhinoceros in their menagerie they might all have used the same cut — a rhino is a rhino, and the engraving indicated that they had one. Of course, there were a few less-than-scrupulous operators who used, say, an engraving showing a troupe of twenty-five elephants when they actually had only three; but such exaggerations were usually forgotten during the excitement of the circus performance.

Most of the circuses which used these cuts are now gone, but the artwork remains as a vivid legacy from one of the most flamboyant and exciting aspects of Americana.

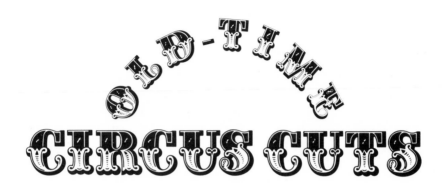

# OLD-TIME CIRCUS CUTS

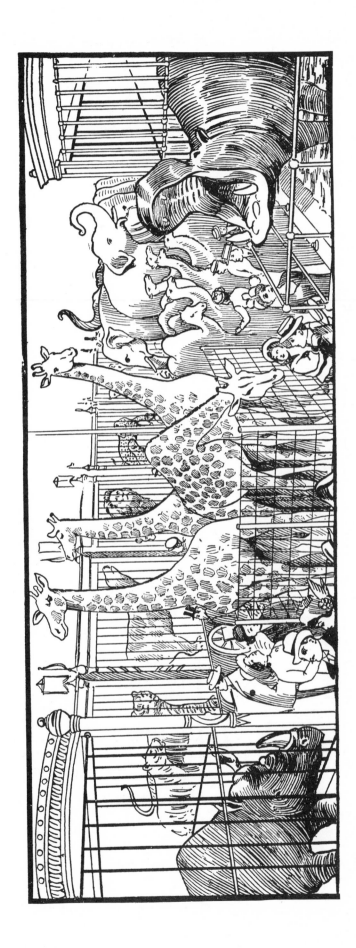

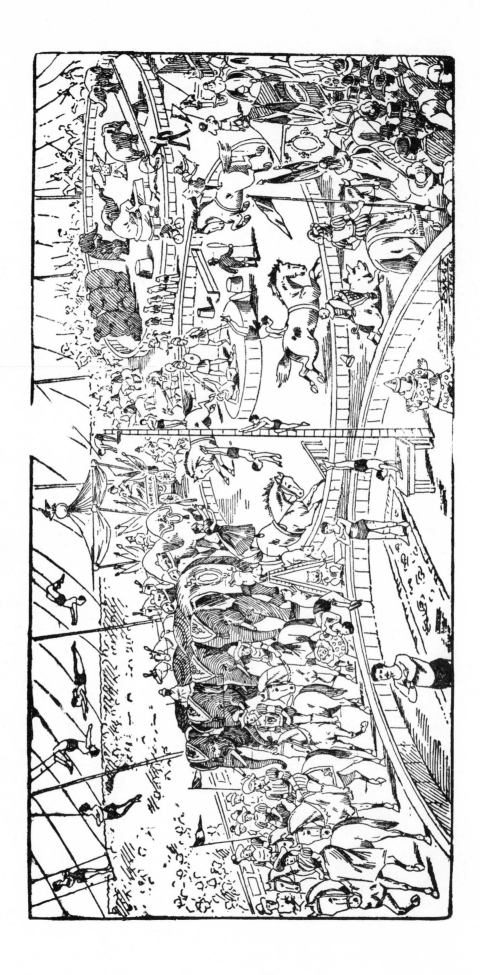

8

11

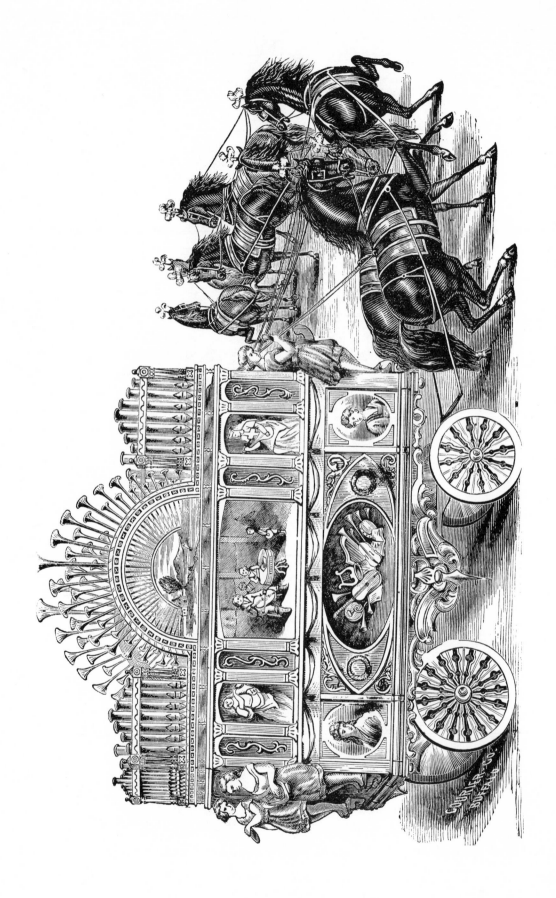

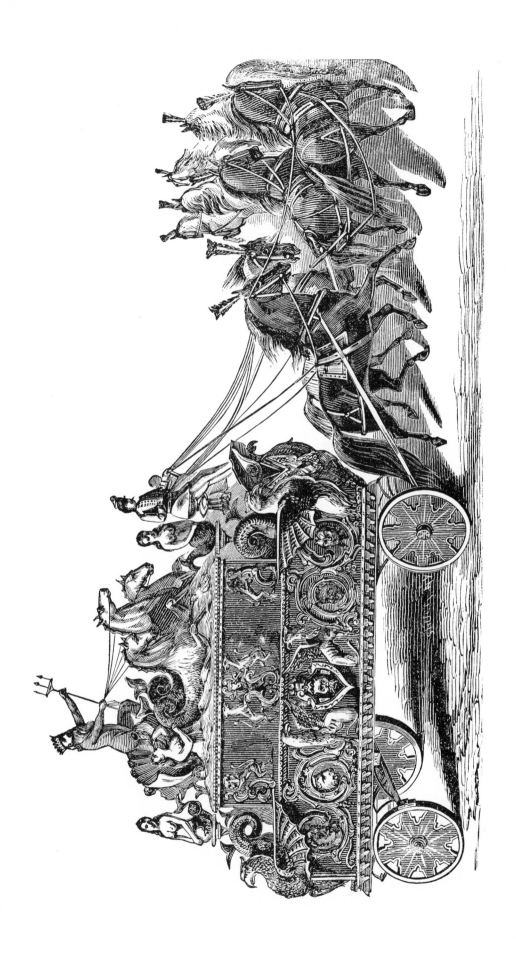

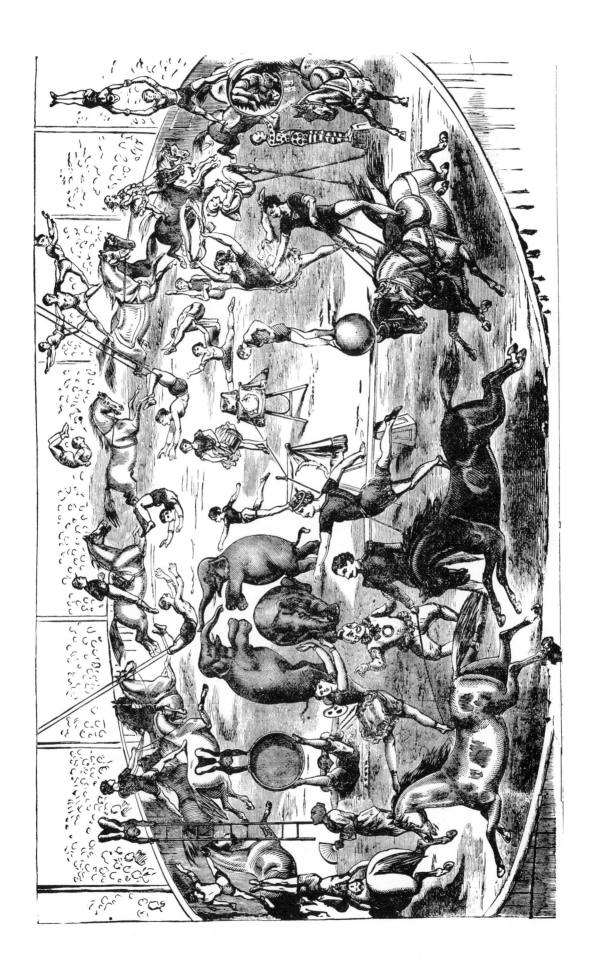

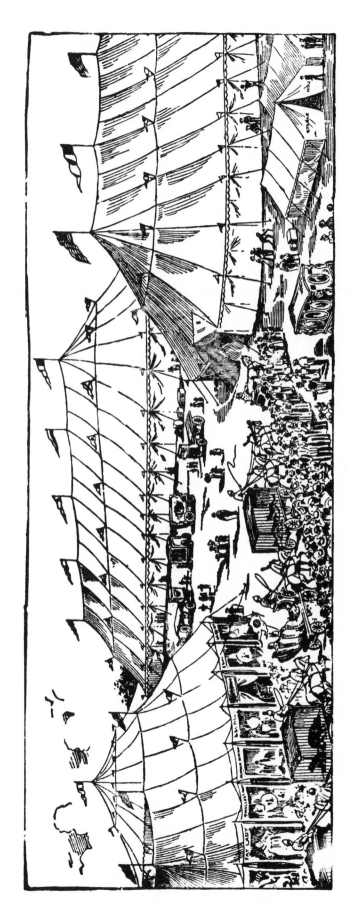

BUFFALO N.Y.

25

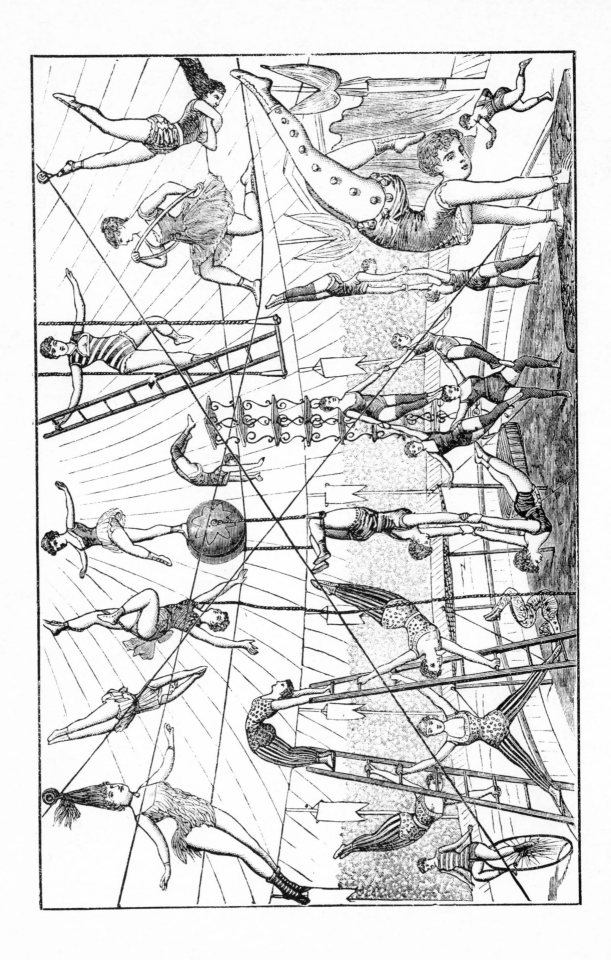

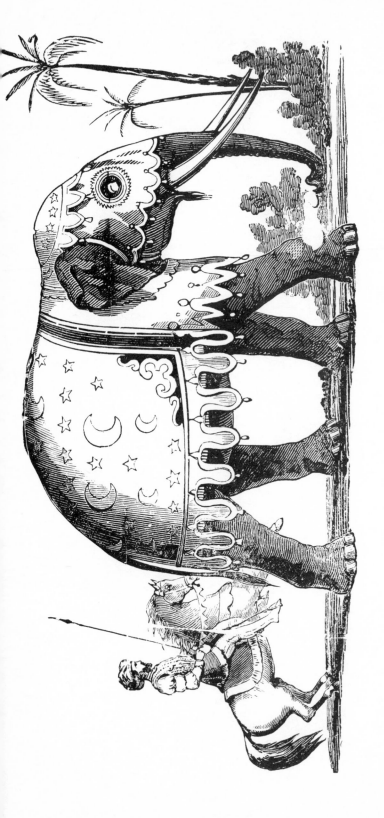

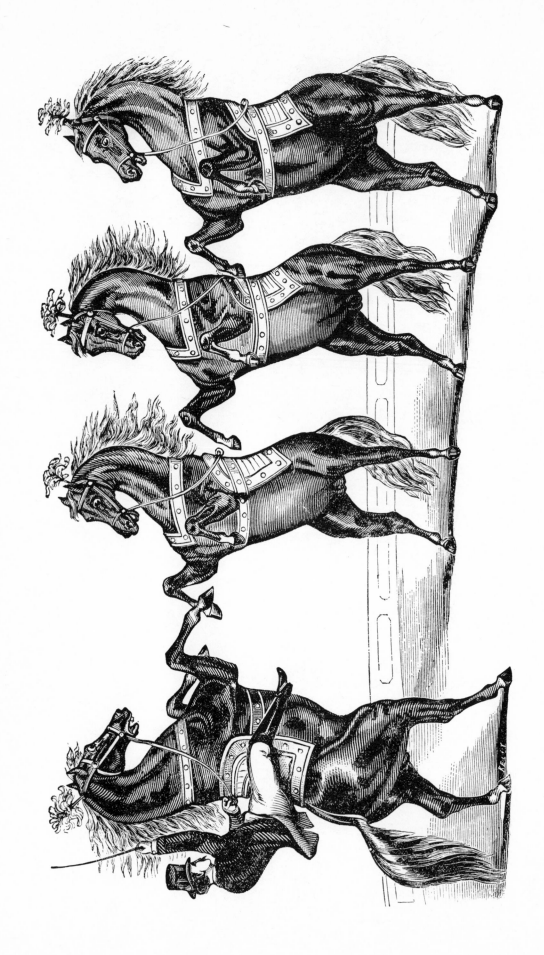

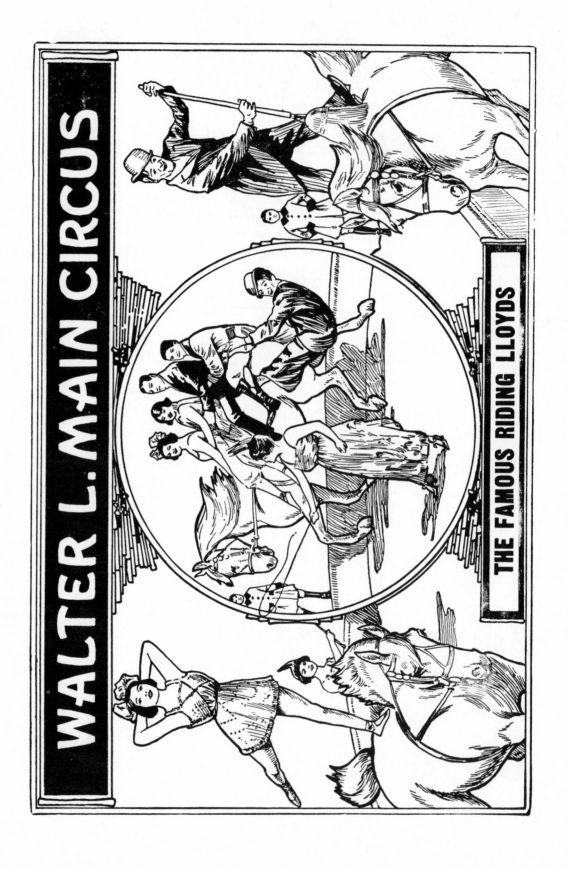

36

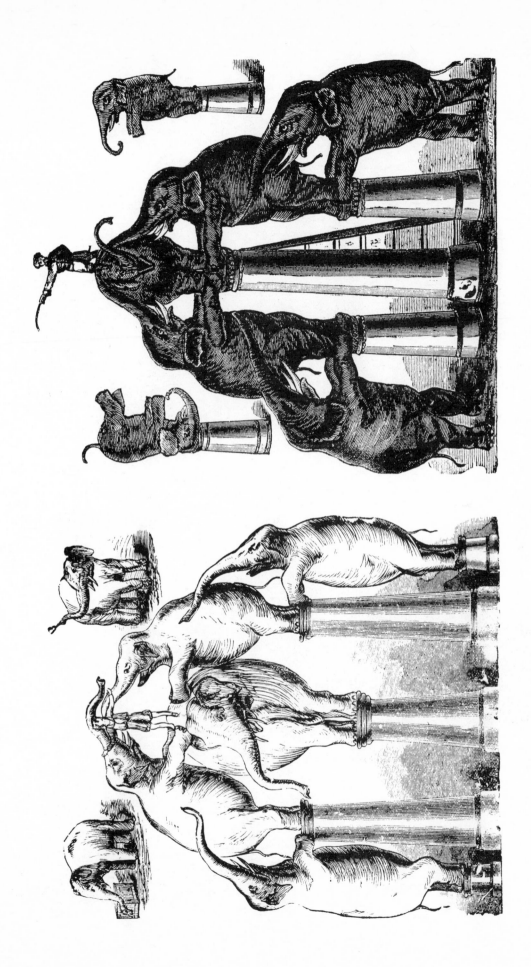

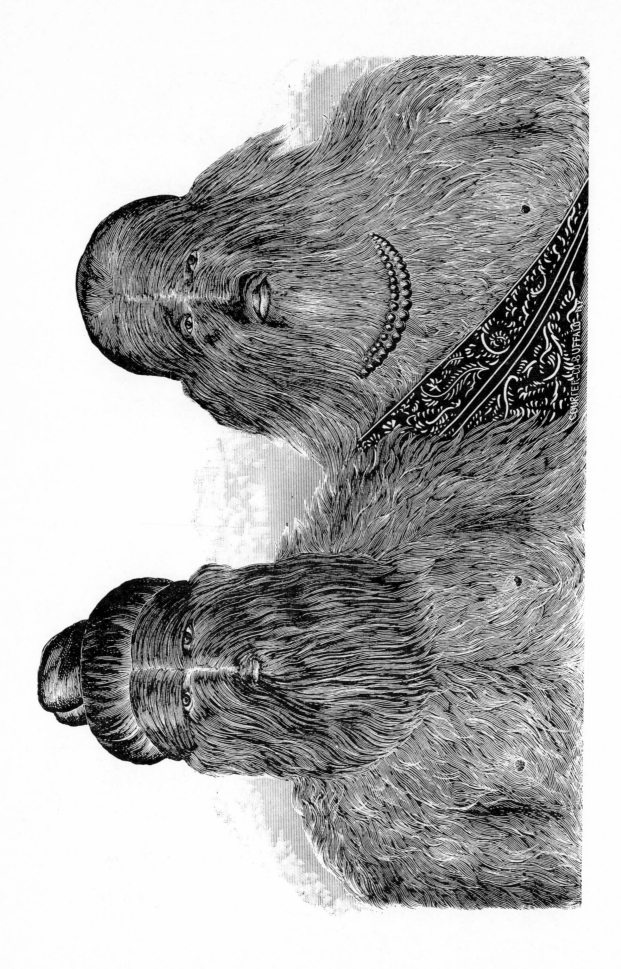

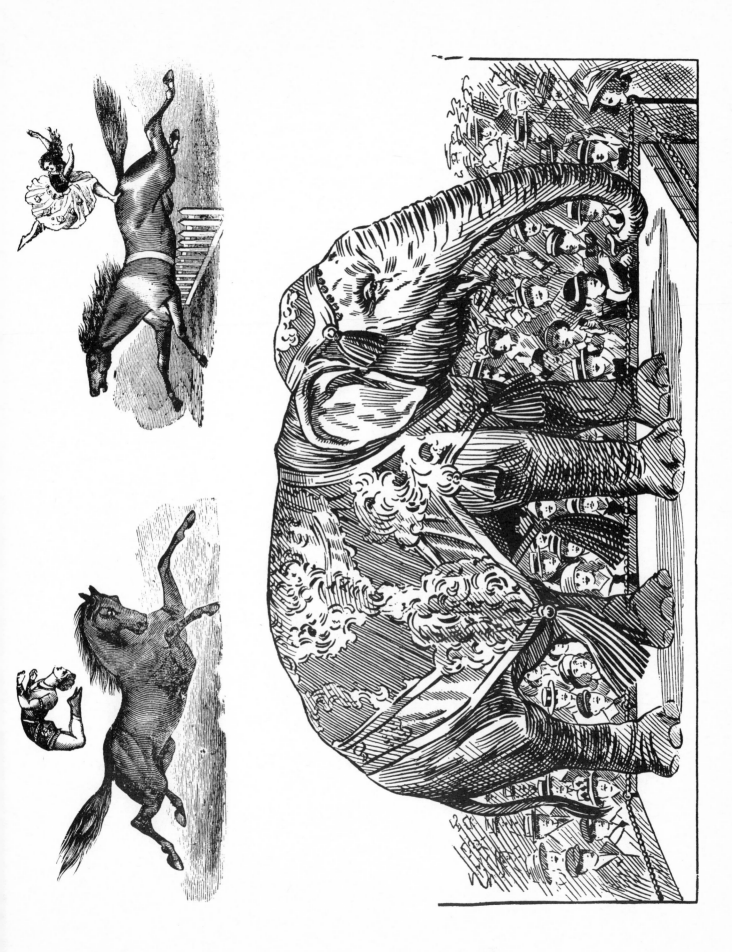

41

THE LARGEST CAMEL IN THE WORLD AS BIG AS AN ELEPHANT

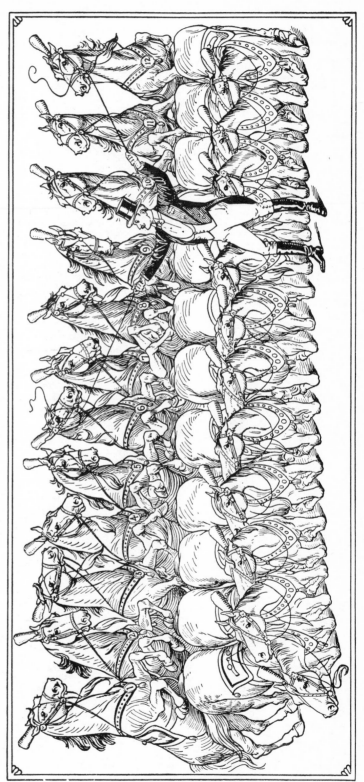

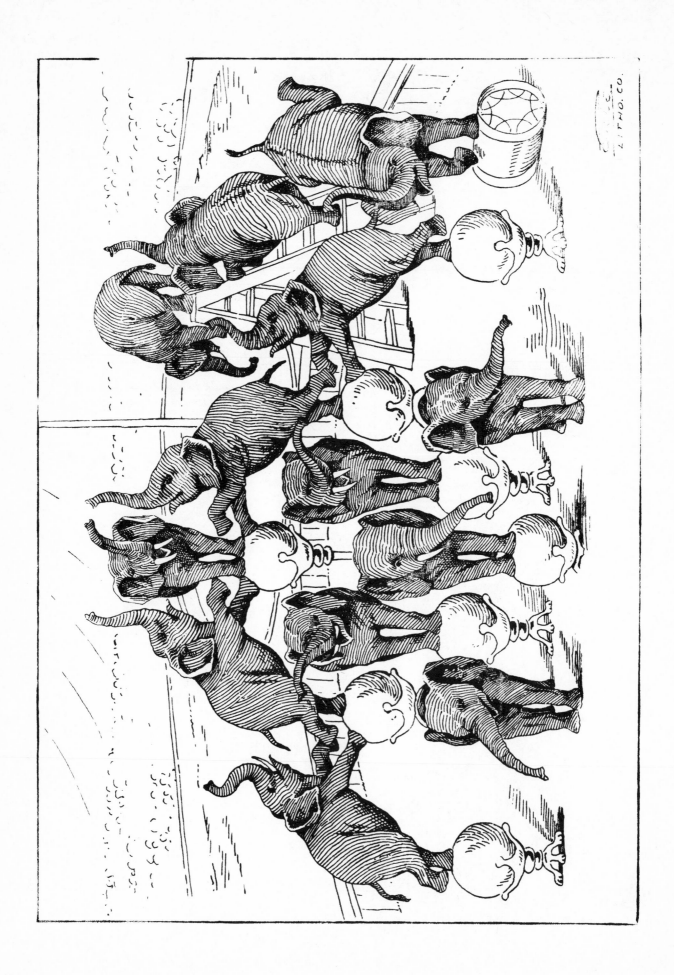

46

48

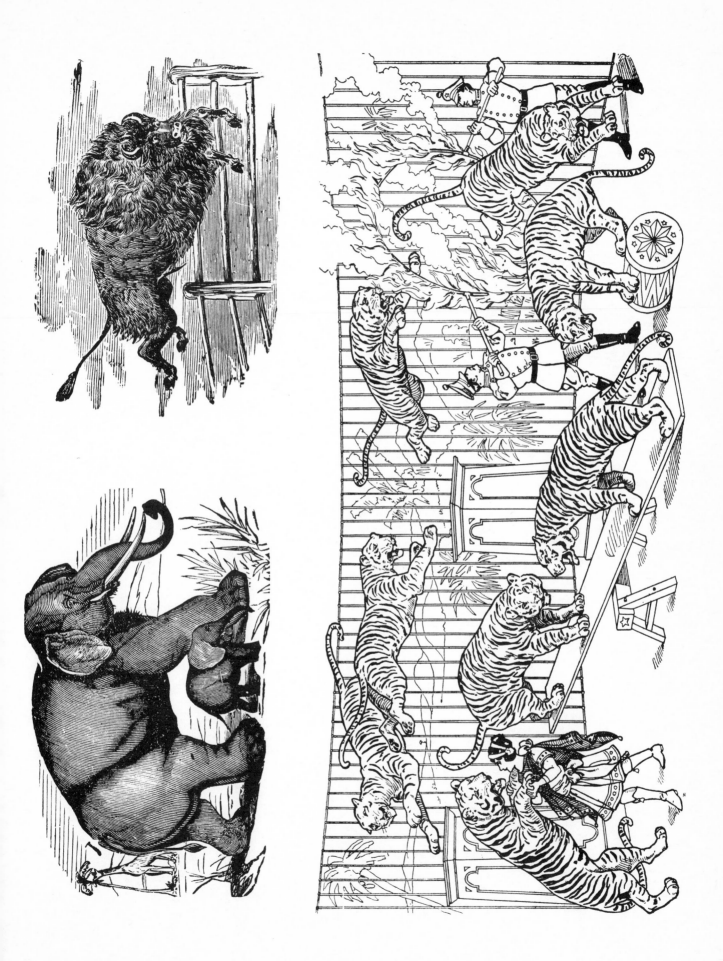

50

ATTRACTION EXTRAORDINARY. A CONGRESS OF JAPANS FAMOUS STRONG MEN, GLADIATORS, SWORDSMEN, WRESTLERS, JIU-JITSU AND ATHLETIC CHAMPIONS.

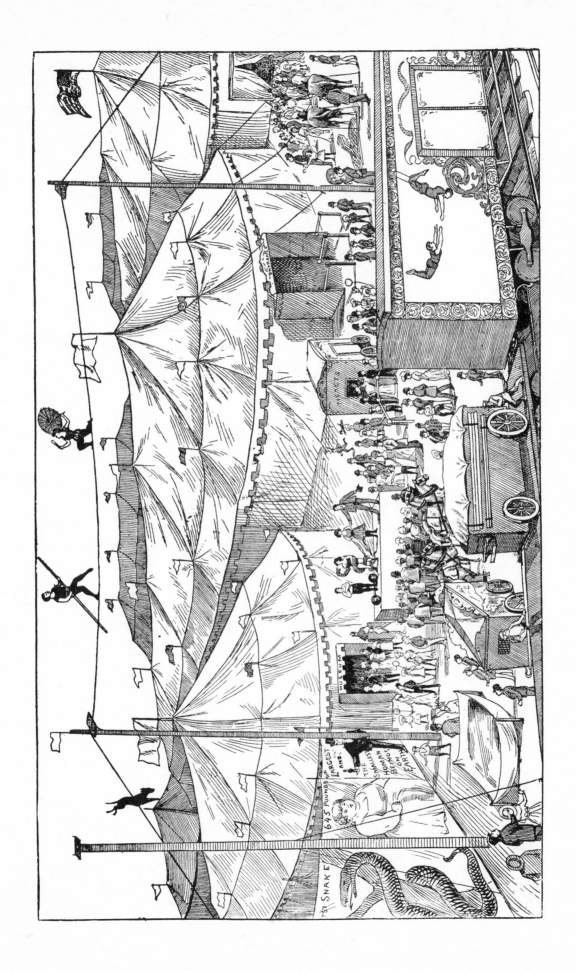

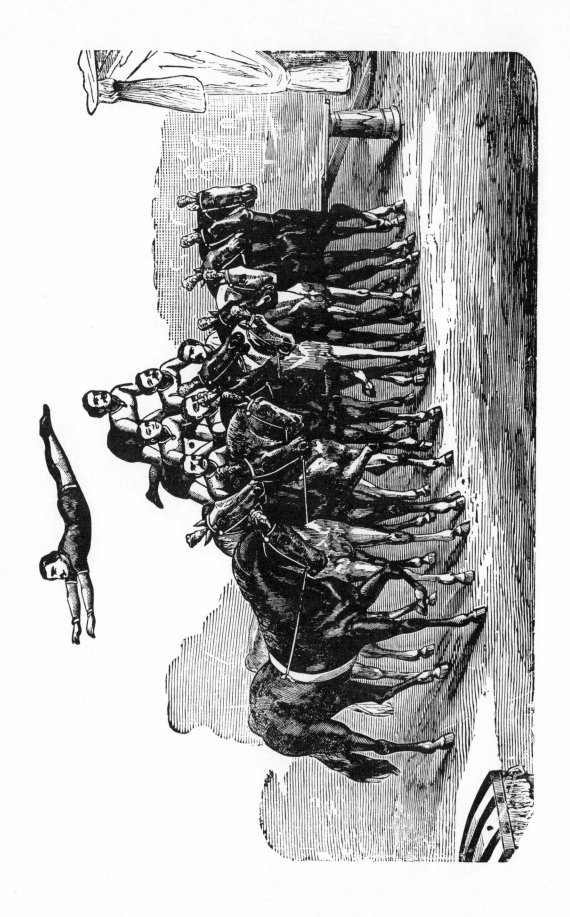

58

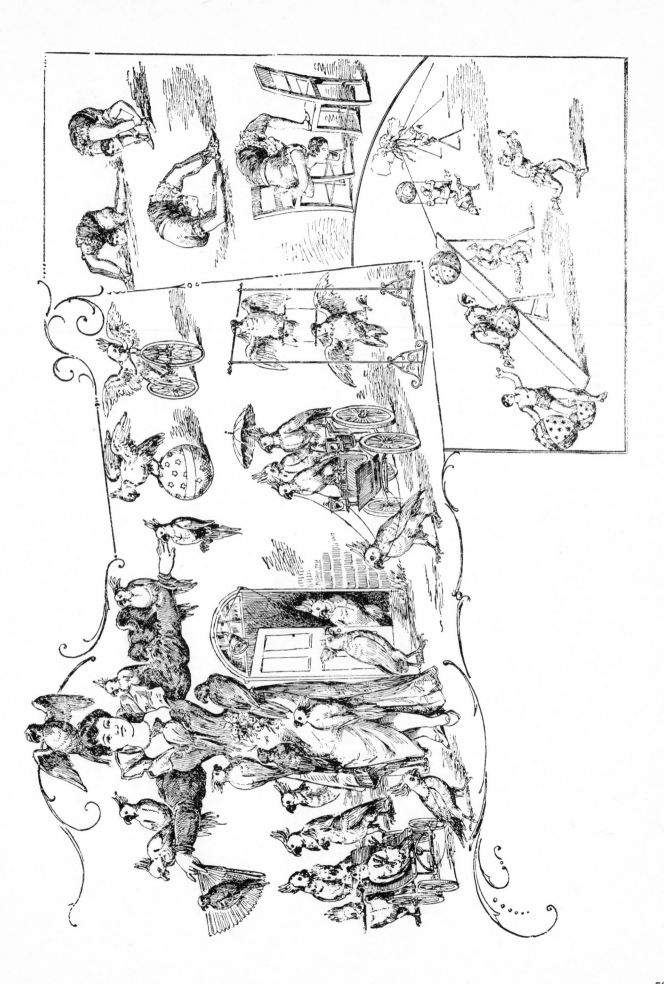

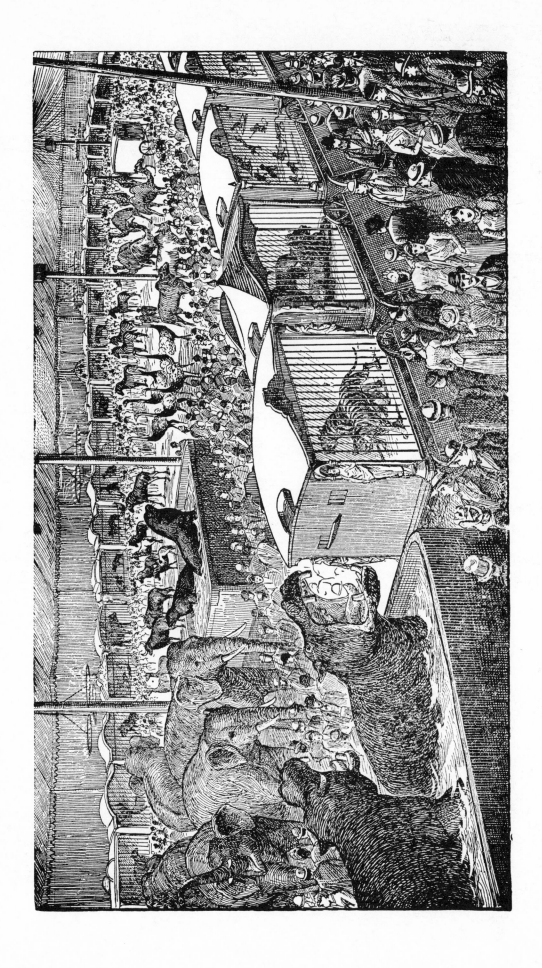

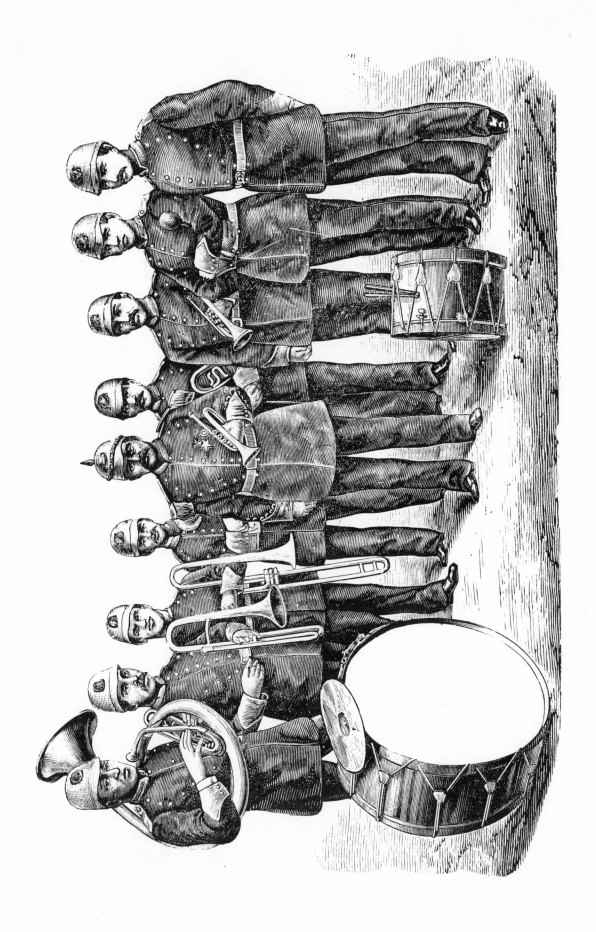

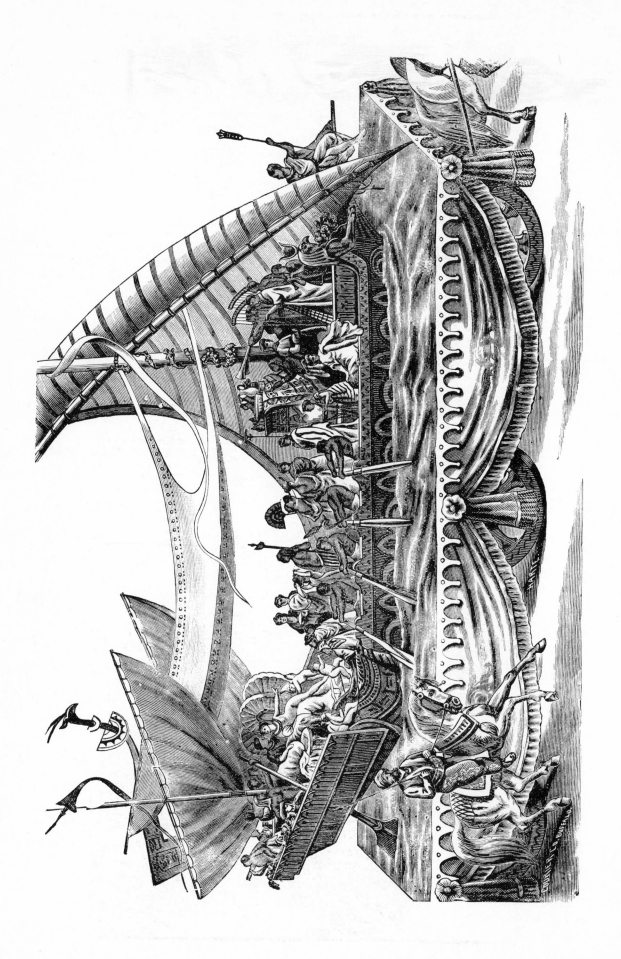

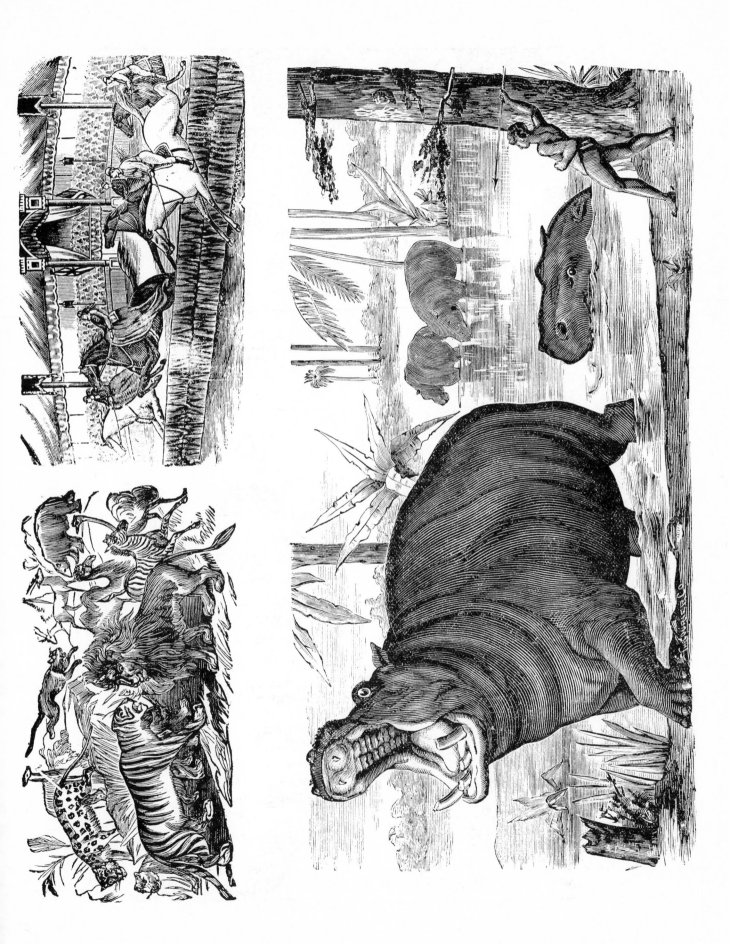

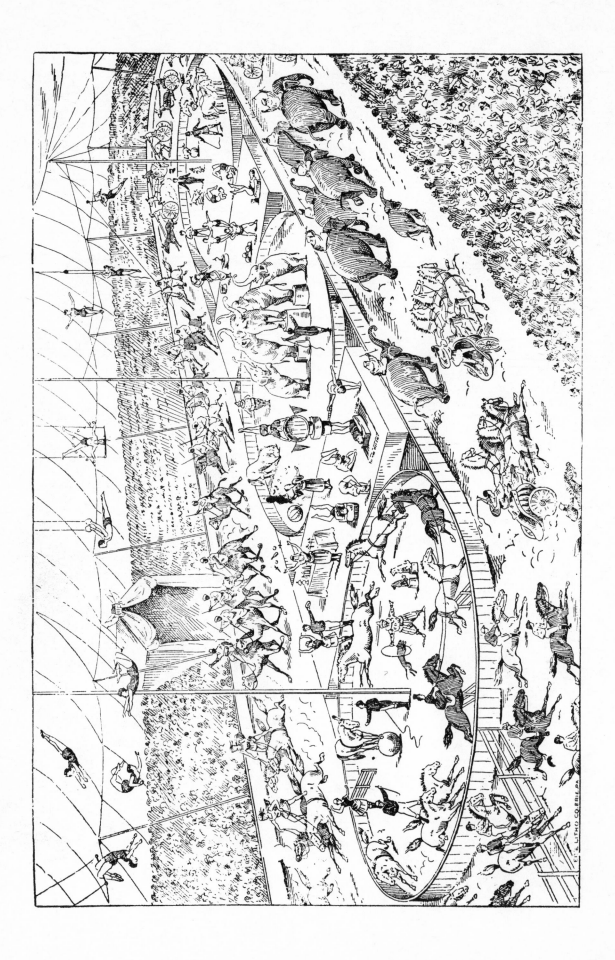

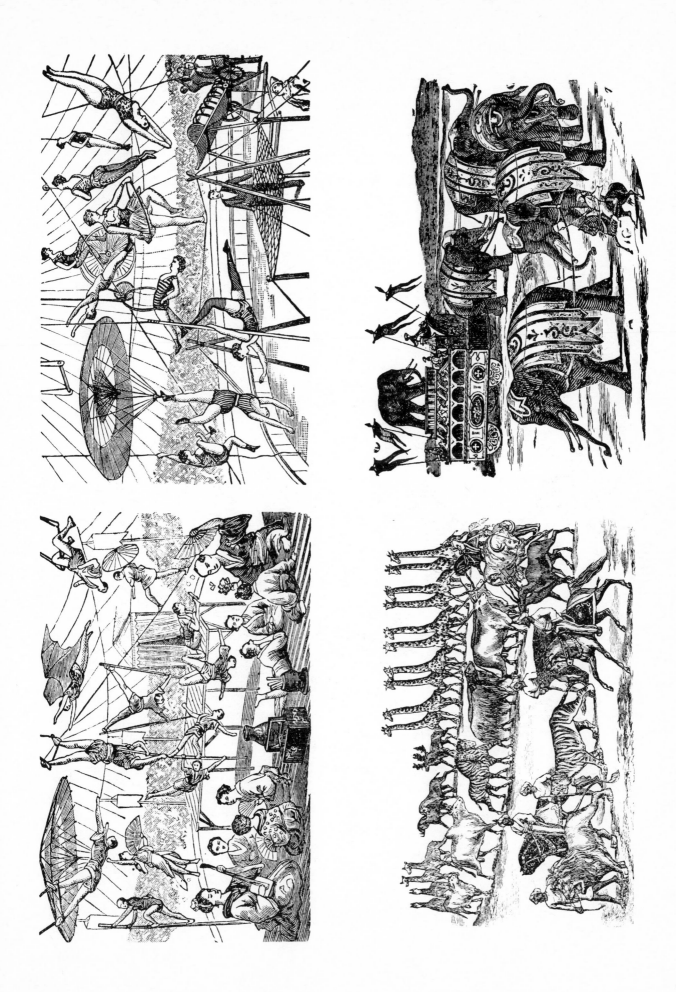

ELEPHANT RACES

80

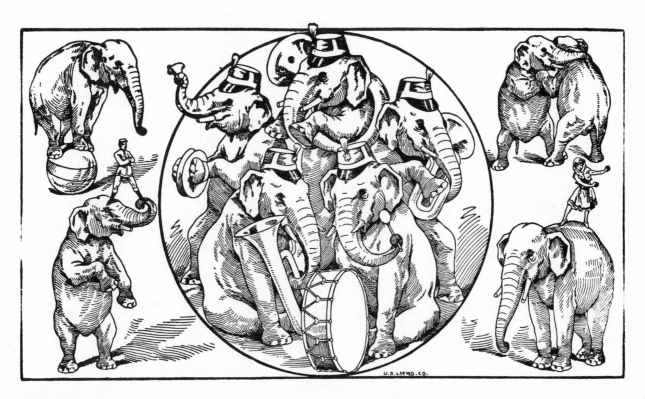

U.S. LITHO. CO.

EVER POPULAR ACTS
BY THE MOST HIGHLY EDUCATED
MAMMOTH PACHYDERM PERFORMERS

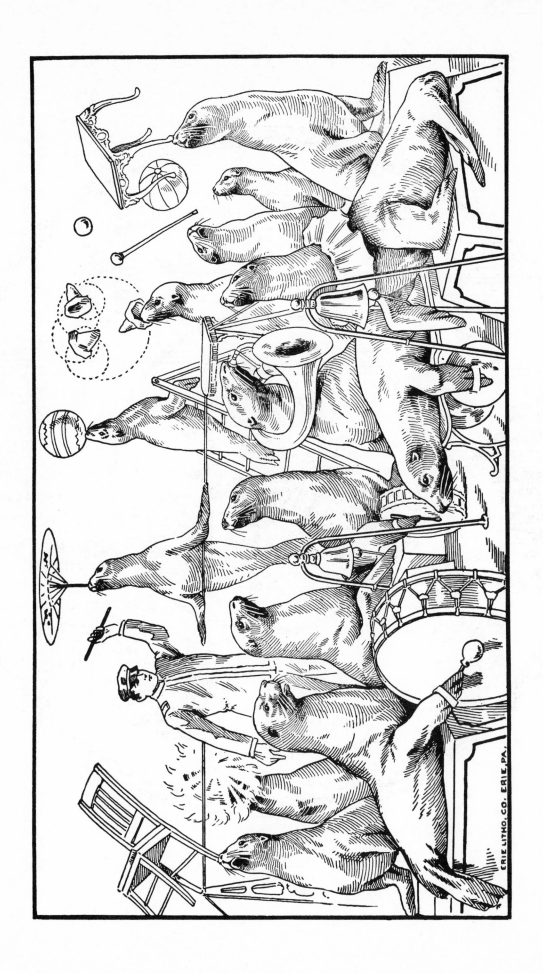

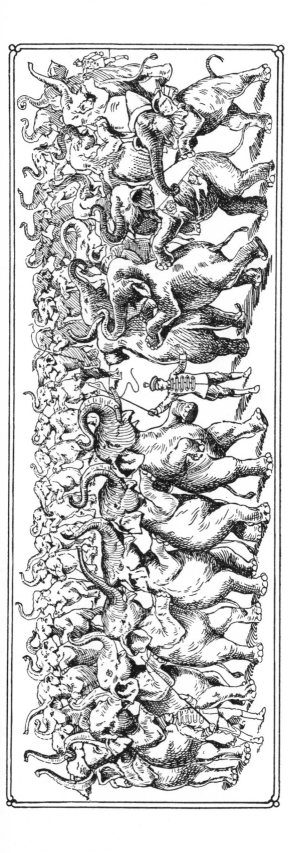

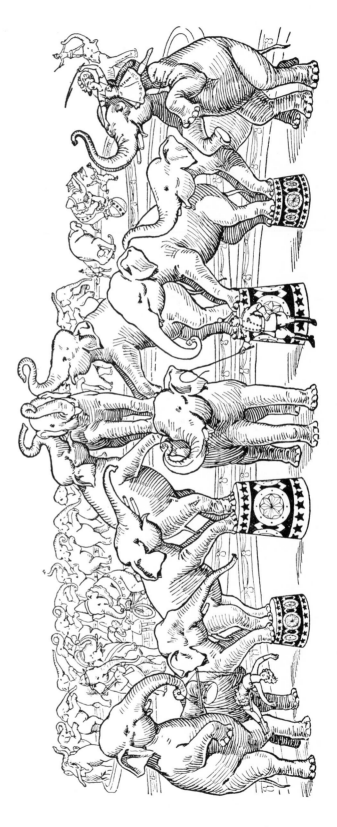

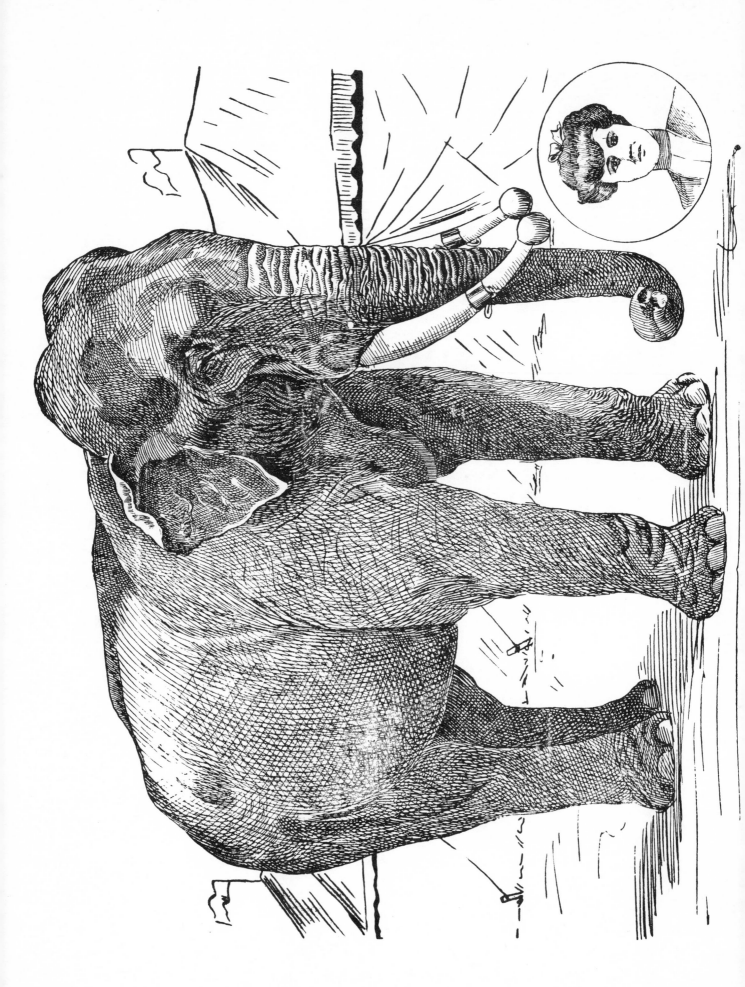

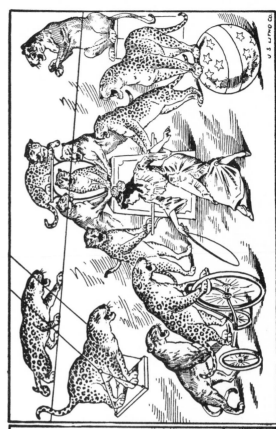

95

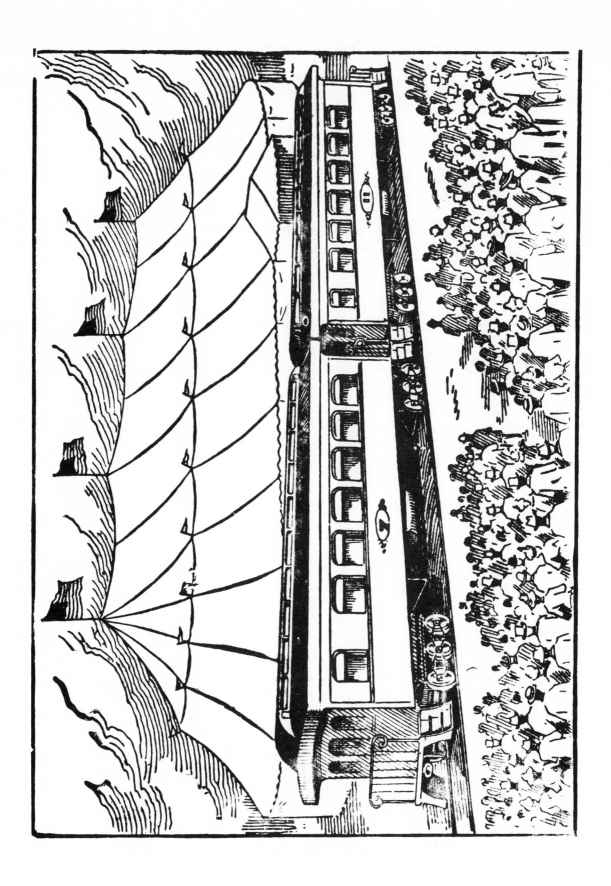

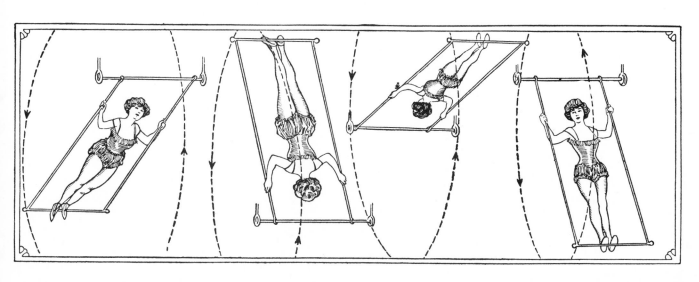

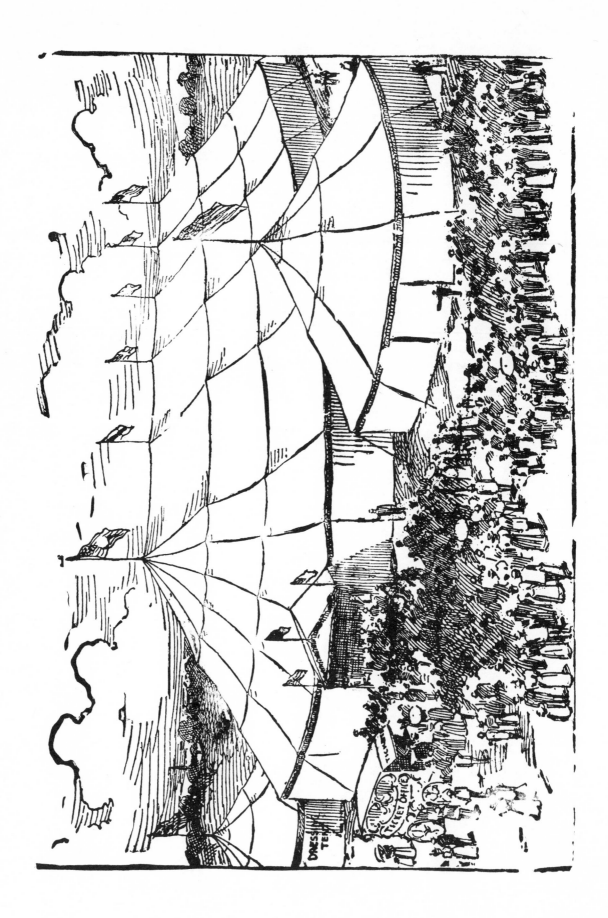

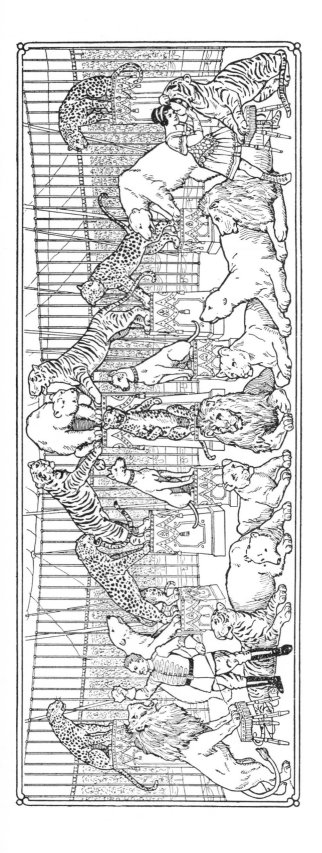

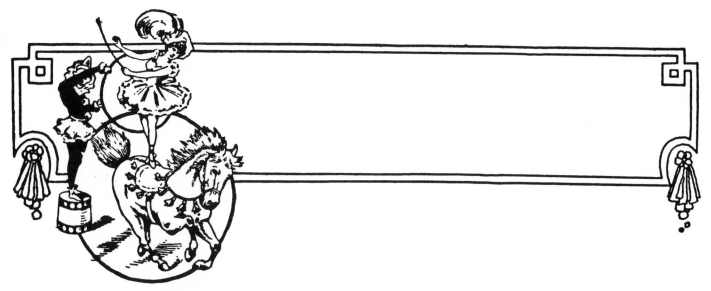

WILD ANIMAL CIRCUS

MAYES.

MAYES.

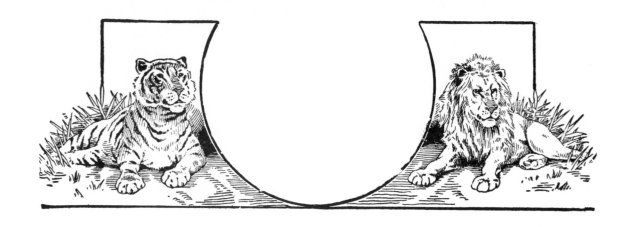

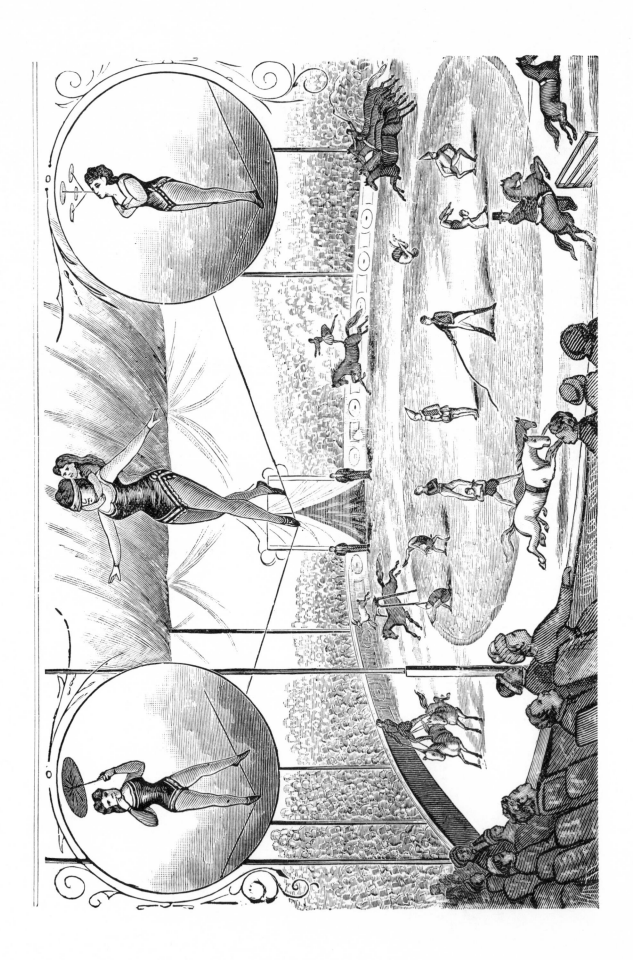